GOD IS BIGGER THAN WE THINK

Mark W. Wagner

DEDICATION

This book is dedicated to my LGBTQ+ friends who have been misunderstood and marginalized and who are searching for a place to belong.

Know that you will always belong to God.

CONTENTS

ACKNOWLEDGMENTS

Thank you to the many friends and family who have supported us on this journey of discovery. To my editor, Treacy for your dedication to this project, and to Hannah Stout for the wonderful cover design.

Special thanks to my wife who spent countless hours reading and editing these posts and has helped me to remain gracious and patient throughout this crazy adventure.

CHAPTER ONE:

THE ADVENTURE BEGINS

Life's an adventure. This has been my mantra for the past ten years or so. More accurately I might say: Life with God is at times an unpredictable and dramatically unfair adventure. Perhaps you can relate. The ups and downs, the joys and sorrows. This short stay on earth can be brutal for some of us. Well, for all of us really. My wife Kalle and I have certainly experienced deep joy and breathtaking beauty, and we have also felt our share of heartache over the years. I suppose we should be grateful for all of these experiences because they have allowed us to relate to some and to sit with others whose depth of suffering we can only imagine.

These past several years have been a whirlwind. God blew down our little stick-built house and we have watched as God picked up the pieces and replaced it with an unshakable structure on a firmer foundation. We have more questions than ever about what this life is and who this God is. I can honestly say that I've never thought more about the book of Job as I have in the past three years: "Where were you when I laid the foundations of the earth?" Alright, alright, I wasn't around, and I don't know the big plan. I'm but a simple sheep. God is good at wrecking our little stick-built lives. Thankfully, God is also a master at putting the pieces back together.

Someday, you and I can grab coffee and we can swap stories. We can laugh about the wrong turns we've made along the way and the graciousness of our God to never give up on us. We could all write books about our journeys. We all have some little slice of wisdom to share, anyone who's ever been alive can add a chapter to the Big story. If they've been paying any attention that is. I've always believed that I would have something to share someday. I've wanted to write a book for as long as I can remember. I thought someday I'd share stories about all of my international travel, the thousands of people I've met and the amazing lessons I've learned along the way. Maybe someday I'll write that book, but not this time.

The adventure I'm about to share with you was completely unexpected and has felt a bit unfair. You see, I have grown up in a certain faith tradition, in a certain culture, in a postmodern American middle-class world, with a world view shaped by my gender, race, socio-economic status, and entitlement that comes with all the unique privileges afforded by those things. My particular growing up experience has formed within me certain cultural biases and stereotypes, some of which I've spent the past ten years trying to unlearn. Many of these factors have contributed to the development of a clouded lens through which I have viewed the world and others. This perspective has at times prevented me from seeing God in all God's beauty and from seeing God in others. This is where our story begins — with my own failure to see.

We all have a lens through which we view the world and others. Our individual filter is defined by things like our culture of origin, socio-economic status, gender, ethnicity, and political views. These things build the foundation for our personal convictions, ideologies and philosophies. But this lens is not sufficient. We must add a new filter through which we view the world. One that is much larger and clearer. This new lens is a mosaic of sorts. One that holds our experiences loosely, with room to grow and an openness to new perspectives. Let's call this the "God-lens." The amazing thing is, God is much bigger and more beautiful and more diverse than we could ever think or imagine.

You see, somewhere along the way I forgot that God is bigger than the Bible, that God is bigger than our faith traditions, and that God is bigger than me. I had forgotten that God is capable of transforming my biblical interpretation. God has given me new eyes through which to view the world and others. It's easy to ignore the fact that Christ is alive and ultimately gets the Final Word. In fact, Christ is the supreme authority over all things, including the Bible. Sometimes it's convenient to rely on our own biblical knowledge and the ability to proof-text certain verses from scripture to support our theological arguments and cultural biases. This is a mistake because this was never how the Bible was intended to be used.

The Bible is the written account of the ancient Jewish and Christian people and their inspired experience of God. The Bible is the written revelation of God, filtered through the human capacity to hear from and understand God. One of my favorite Biblical scholars, Richard Rohr likes to say that the Bible is the word of God in the words of men. In other words, the authors of the Biblical text were regular people like you and me. They wrote from a particular place in history, saw through a particular cultural and socio-economic lens, and they had a limited understanding of biology, psychology and ecology. They were primarily concerned with telling their version of who God is and who they were.

Thus, we now read and interpret Scripture through our own historical-cultural lens. This doesn't mean the Bible has nothing to offer us in how we should live our lives, but it does require a greater understanding of the historical and cultural context within which the Scriptures were written in order to faithfully and responsibly apply them today. When we do not have a firm grasp on what the Bible is and how the Bible should be used, humans tend to misuse the Biblical text, extracting individual verses in the Bible to support and defend our own personal ideologies or political positions. History has proven that this type of Biblical interpretation causes immense harm (e.g. slavery, divorce, etc...). So how then should we read and interpret Scripture so as not to cause harm to others? Well, a good place to start would be to examine how Jesus himself interpreted the Scriptures.

In John 5:39, Jesus reminds the religious leaders that they will not find Truth in the Scriptures, but the purpose of the Scriptures themselves are to point to the person of Jesus Christ! Therefore, we must read and interpret all of the sacred scriptures through the lens of the life and ministry of Jesus Christ. All of history is moving from, towards and in Christ, who is fully God and fully human. So, how did Jesus treat people? What did Jesus teach? What does Jesus have to say about the nature and characteristics of God? Oh yeah, we can't forget the presence and inspiration of the Holy Spirit, constantly guiding and shepherding us towards a fuller understanding of who God is. This is how our journey began; the Holy Spirit guiding us as we sought a bigger view of God and the Bible.

When Kalle and I began to investigate our own beliefs around the topic of lesbian, gay, bisexual, trans-gender and queer (LGBTQ+) inclusion in the Evangelical church, we were pretty convinced that our lens was the correct lens. I could quote the seven verses in scripture that backed up my own cultural biases and the stereotypes that had developed from my decades of growing up in conservative Christian America. I had subscribed to the narrow views of Evangelicalism, and I was well-versed in the nuances of how I should explain to someone why evangelicals excluded LGBTQ+ individuals. In the past several years, however, God has deconstructed these arguments one by one.

What we discovered is that God had a new

lens for us to see through. God has given us the opportunity to learn and to see in new ways. The beautiful thing is that God never forced us to try on these new lenses. God does not force us to do anything. God invites us to Godself. God invites us to know more fully, to love more passionately, to feel more deeply, and to see more clearly.

Ultimately, Kalle and I decided that we didn't have all the answers, so we chose to accept God's invitation with open hearts and minds. We chose to consider a new perspective, to take up the call that God placed on our lives to begin a journey of discovery that would ultimately lead to transformation. We extend this invitation to you. Embark on this journey of discovery with us and hopefully you will be led to a deeper love for others and a bigger view of God.

* In an effort to protect the privacy of those people involved in our journey, I've changed some of the names. Also, in an attempt to keep things short and sweet, neat and tidy, the timeline of events has been adjusted slightly.

CHAPTER TWO:

ROOTS

The small Southern church I grew up in always taught me two things: Jesus is Lord and the Bible is God's word and our final authority and guide in this life. Of those two things I was certain. You can visit most Evangelical churches in America today and those two foundational principles will most likely be posted as an icon on the Sunday morning bulletin or painted as a mural on some concrete block wall in the fellowship hall. These two generalizations are central to the Evangelical tradition, and I've never questioned them. These two principles helped shape my faith as a child and into High School.

When I finished High School, I was already writing songs and traveling a bit around the Southeast performing at large churches. I knew I would be famous someday like Bebo Norman or Brandon Heath, traveling the world as a musician-ary (get it? Musician + missionary). I went to college near Nashville with every intention of being "discovered," knowing I would quickly sign a record deal, and thinking I would then go on to record several Grammy-winning albums. Most days I would spend several hours designing the album covers in my head, thinking through what kind of blazer I would be wearing in the photo shoot. I knew after 10-12 years as an artist I would then produce albums for younger artists, building my catalogue of hit songs and ultimately growing my own nest-egg with hundreds of "screen songs" that would be sung in churches across America each week.

Most of the concerts I performed throughout college and beyond were in partnership with Young Life, one of the largest non-denominational Evangelical youth organizations in the world. I played at countless Young Life camps, banquets, local club gatherings and events from 2005-2018. Not to mention serving on Young Life committees, working as a volunteer leader in Tennessee and Washington and ultimately going on full-time staff in Utah for a few years. Most of my best friends are either on Young Life staff, have been on Young Life staff, or currently serve as volunteer Young Life leaders. Needless to say, I am intimately connected with the organization of Young Life, and I have a deep love and appreciation for the way they walk alongside young people, sharing the Gospel in word and deed. My own life was transformed by my Young Life leaders in High School. Young Life helped shape my faith and my theology throughout High School and college.

Upon graduating from Middle Tennessee State Univ. with a degree in music business and spending three years traveling the world and writing what I hoped would be the next hit song, I realized that God was up to something. I had the sense that God was nudging me in a different direction. I would leave songwriting sessions with famous songwriters who had written major hits in Christian music and feel sick to my stomach. I was moving towards my dream, but it felt like I was running away from God. That's when my life took a drastic turn.

The year was 2007 and the weather was hot and humid, as most summer days in Tennessee are. I sat down for coffee with my "unofficial" A&R guy, his name was *literally* Guy. He is still a good friend, and I've always appreciated his support and honesty. That day I hit him with a bit of a surprise. "Guy, I'm pretty sure God wants me to go to Seminary." He looked confused. He had spent the past several weeks setting up writing appointments for me with other signed artists and writers. We were hopefully moving towards a record deal with plans for a bright future. "I have no idea why," I said. "But I'm pretty sure I need to move to the West Coast and continue my theological education." I was convinced God just wanted to give me a more solid foundation of Biblical knowledge, so that when I stood in front of crowds of millions of people performing my latest hit song I wouldn't look like an idiot. I convinced Guy of this too and that was that.

I packed my bags and headed off to Fuller Theological Seminary three months later, where I began the next chapter of my educational journey. Fuller is the largest Seminary in the world and one of the most diverse. I loved sitting in classrooms with students from every denomination, representing sometimes over 10 countries in one class session. This made for some interesting discussions. At the very least my narrow Southern Evangelical theology and world-view began to expand. Traveling internationally during this season also helped.

While in Seminary I was still traveling full-time as a singer-songwriter. I've had the incredible privilege of traveling to 15 countries and most states in the US sharing my music, and I've sold an estimated 60,000 albums internationally. I've written hundreds of songs with countless other co-writers, and I've produced eight albums (all in Nashville) with three different producers. This extensive travel and work as a songwriter, coupled with the countless relationships I've built along the way, has had a significant impact on my understanding of who God is and who I am.

In between my travels I was sitting in week-long intensives as a seminary student and participating in online discussion boards and video conferences. There were even times when I would participate in online discussions moments before playing a concert. All of this travel and all of the new relationships I've built along the way has led to a deeper view of who God is, one that is far removed from my perspective as a young I Southern Baptist from East Tennessee.

After graduating from Fuller with a Master of Arts in Theology and Ministry I went to work for Youth for Christ. I worked there for one year in downtown Seattle, overseeing an urban youth program of which I was already intimately connected. After 12 months, I handed off the baton of leadership to one of my friends from the neighborhood where I worked with young people, and he promptly ran with it, accomplishing much more than I ever could have. Oh yeah, it was a few years before this that I got married (That was awesome).

Kalle and I said "I do" in June of 2011. Then, six months after we were married, we packed up our lives and moved back to Nashville to begin working with an old friend who was doing extensive development work and theological training throughout Africa. We would spend the next five years working in some capacity with this organization, raising awareness and funds for their child scholarship program. In 2016, I began to recognize God's hand guiding us into a new season. We both sensed God moving us towards working directly with young people, not just singing and telling stories about it. That's about the time our journey working with college students began.

Looking back, I can see the countless ways that God has prepared us for this mission of telling people the truth about who Jesus is, and I literally wouldn't change one thing about our crazy journey. Each move, each school, each country, each relationship has taught us something new about who God is and who we are. Each step along the journey has prepared us for the next one. However, nothing could have prepared me for the conversations I was about to start having with LGBTQ+ students in our college congregation. These students were wrestling with one question: 'How can I have faith in God when the church says I don't fully belong?' But, I'm getting ahead of myself...

CHAPTER THREE:

A NEW EDUCATION

In 2017 I began my Doctoral studies at Boston University. This meant two things primarily: First that I was going back to school and second that I would be going to school in Boston. I was excited for the opportunity to further my theological education at Boston University, one of the most prestigious Universities in the world. Early in my program I was encouraged to choose a focus for my research, and I chose the obvious topic: developing a holistic theology of worship. More specifically, I would focus on the intersection of worship and justice. I had been writing and recording music professionally for over 12 years, as well as working as an artist advocate promoting orphan education in Africa, so this seemed like the perfect platform for me to base my Doctoral research on.

At the time I began this program I was working full-time on staff with Young Life in Utah while still traveling part-time around the country performing at churches and in other Young Life arenas. Kalle was on staff with me, and together we were leading Young Life College at the University of Utah. We both love the mission of Young Life: To introduce young people to Jesus Christ and help them grow in their faith. We are passionate about this mission, as both our lives had been transformed through the ministry of Young Life during our youth. I knew my Doctoral work would contribute to our work with college students in Utah and my work as a recording artist. Things were lining up perfectly as I prepared for my first week-long intensive on campus.

We traveled to Boston, in August 2017, where I would spend 10 days sitting in a classroom of fellow full-time ministry professionals. I woke early on our first morning there and went for a long run along the Charles River to clear my head. I was nervous and excited to begin this new educational journey; I would never have guessed how much of an adventure this would be.

This particular class would be fun, as we were learning how to apply transformational leadership concepts in our own ministry contexts. I had a pretty good grasp on the content of the class from the reading I had done before arriving in Boston. I thought I knew just what to expect. I could recite from memory the concepts from our pre-class reading, and I was looking forward to sharing how I'd already been applying these concepts in my own ministry back in Utah.

That first morning of class we had a surprise guest lecturer named David who had come to share about his own journey of transformation as a

Methodist Minister. Our professor shared that David had served as a Methodist minister for close to 30 years. He's a brilliant man, talented and passionate about pastoral ministry. He was visiting our class to share about some of the unique challenges he had faced in his life and ministry. As David shared, I could tell immediately that this was a sophisticated and intelligent man who loved teaching. But more than that I could sense David's deep love of the Lord and his love for pastoral ministry.

He smiled as he boasted about his wife and children, and he shared openly about his background and experience of being called into full-time pastoral ministry. I was inspired and encouraged. He spoke for almost half an hour about his experience growing up and wrestling with his own faith and identity as a child of God. I admired him for his strength and courage as he shared about trying to follow Christ throughout High School. Our experiences had many similarities, and I was already thinking how great it would be to grab coffee with David after class and hear more about his journey and call into ministry. David paused and took a sip of coffee. He then looked up at our professor, searching for some sign of affirmation before he continued sharing. That's when he said it: "I knew from an early age that I was a boy living in a girl's body."

David shared openly that he had undergone a transitional procedure earlier in life to become a male. This was a shock for me and even more shocking as I reflected on his 30 years of serving as a pastor in the United Methodist Church (UMC) as a trans-gender person. I slumped down in my chair and took a deep breath. How could a transgender person be allowed to serve as the senior pastor of a church? Who would allow this? Did anyone else know? Was this his 'coming out'? Shouldn't we report this to someone? He went on to share that in 2009 he had "come out" to his congregation and was in the process of publishing a book about his journey. Though he received an immense amount negative feedback from a lot of people, his own congregation embraced him, and he was able to keep his job in the UMC. Wait. What? Why wasn't he fired immediately?

I looked around the room as David continued to share. My palms were starting to sweat, I started getting a little nervous. Didn't David know that he was speaking to a classroom of Doctor of Christian Ministry students? Didn't he realize that we were all *Christians* and that we all held fast to the authority of scripture which clearly states that his choice to transition was a sin? Certainly, everyone else in the room *must* have been feeling the same way. I snuck a peek at Jeff, my closest friend in the program who was a pastor at a large church in Texas at the time. He and I had never talked explicitly about the LGBTQ+ issue, but I knew his church was fairly conservative. He must have been feeling the same way...right? But, he looked calm and composed. Way to go, Jeff. Good for you. I'm sure I was starting to sweat through my shirt at this point. I looked behind me where my professor was sitting. Surely, she was preparing to stop David and take control of the situation. How would she clean up this mess? Shockingly, she was *smiling*! What was happening?

Confused and unnerved, I began to try and calm myself down. I had learned some deep breathing exercises in yoga that I tried to put into practice. Deep breath, long exhale, deep breath, long exhale, and hold. Thoughts were racing through my mind as I realized that no one else in the room appeared shaken. No one *else* in the room was sweating! Was I the only one that was listening? David was spilling his guts about how he had been treated so poorly by Christians, judged and condemned because of his choice to change genders. In my head I was thinking, "Well, it *is* sin and you are living in *unrepentant* sin. It's our job as Christian ministers to help you understand the implications of this decision." Was I off base here? Suddenly, I felt like maybe *I* was the odd man out. Was I the only one in this room that felt this way?

My mind was racing with questions. I was struggling to understand David's story and how he could be serving as a Christian minister. He shared for almost two hours about the ways God had met him in his struggle with gender identity. He had learned that God was bigger than gender, and through his story he had been able to minister to hundreds of other Christians who had their own struggles with sexuality. David shared openly and honestly about his passion for God and for the church. I could clearly see that he was a man after God's own heart; but he was also *transgender*.

That night, after I returned back to the dorm, I told Kalle about meeting David. I shared as much of his story as I could remember, and she was just as shocked as I had been. We talked for hours about our own beliefs around the issue of LGBTQ+ individuals and how, or if, they ought to be allowed to serve in the church. I had always been taught that homosexuality or transgenderism was a sin, and that any person who had *chosen* to live this "lifestyle" should not be allowed to serve in the church. But was that really what I *believed*? Was that *really* God's heart?

Kalle and I spent most of our trip back to Utah at the end of that week talking about David and wondering where we stood on this topic. "Why haven't we ever faced this issue in our own Young Life area? I know there is a large population of LGBTQ+ people in Salt Lake City," I said. "Why don't they come to Young Life? I mean Young Life's tagline is *Every kid, everywhere, for eternity*!" Kalle listened intently, and I could see the wheels spinning in her head. "Don't LGBTQ+ students know they're *invited*," she asked? "I mean what is Young Life's stance anyway? We don't really talk about this issue during our staff meetings." I reached for my phone and searched online for Young Life's official policy. I had to do a little digging on the Young Life website, but I finally found their policy on LGBTQ+ inclusion. The policy basically states that LGBTQ+ individuals are welcome to *attend* Young Life meetings and events, but they cannot serve in a position of leadership, be on staff, or volunteer at any camps. Well, I guess they're *mostly* invited.

CHAPTER FOUR:

TRANSITION

Transition is never easy, but it can *always* be good. What I mean is, although change can be hard and unexpected, we will eventually find the good in whatever new adventure lies ahead. A year prior to beginning my studies in Boston, in the summer of 2016, Kalle and I found out some difficult news that would alter the future of our family: we would not be able to have our own children.

I'll never forget that hot August day in Salt Lake City when I went to retrieve the results of my "fertility test." Which, by the way, if there are any guys out there reading this that have had to take a "fertility test," I feel you. This particular test may have been the most awkward event of my adult life, but a necessary step in our investigative effort to determine why we had not been able to get pregnant after four years of trying to conceive. The results were clear: according to the test (multiple tests actually) there would be no chance for us to conceive a child.

* Sidenote: If this is similar to your own story and you've been struggling with infertility, I can relate to your pain. I also understand the frustration when people say things like: "Don't give up hope. God can do anything. There's a miracle out there waiting for you." Blah, blah, blah. Yeah, I know that God is bigger than infertility, but sometimes we aren't quite ready to hear that. Sometimes we just need to hurt for a while.

I left the doctor's office and went straight to my favorite restaurant in SLC, East Liberty Tap House. It was 11:30am and I ordered a burger with fries and a cold beer. I needed to "decompress" as they say. A few days later some wise friends helped me understand the reality of the news I'd just received. They encouraged me to take time to "grieve the loss of this dream you've had to have your own children someday" (Thank God for Billy and Katie Tormey).

The realization that we would not be able to conceive gave us clarity on an issue that we had discussed for years. We decided that we would officially begin the adoption process. That's when the barrage of paperwork began, and it still hasn't ended. Honestly, the adoption process can feel like a fiction novel that you begin with excitement, then halfway through it starts to feel a little long and boring, and then near the end you almost stop reading because you can't see how the ending could be worth the journey.

Almost exactly one year after receiving our fertility test results (September 2018) we received a call from an attorney in SLC that had our adoption profile on file: "Hi Mark and Kalle, there is a mom in Idaho that would like to meet you. She has reviewed your file and would like to consider you to adopt her child." This was the miracle we had been praying for.

Two weeks after that call we were on the road driving North to Idaho. We met the mother and had a wonderful weekend together. We immediately began filling out the necessary paperwork. A few weeks after that we learned the gender of the child and had a group of friends over to our house for a "revealing party." I spent an entire Saturday putting together the nursery, building a crib and setting up the glider. Kalle and I planned a baby shower in SLC, her sister planned a party in Washington, and my sister booked the venue for our shower in Tennessee. Things were falling into place and we were so excited.

As I said before, transition is never easy, but it can always be good. On November 2, 2018, two months after we had been selected as adoptive parents for a baby boy in Idaho, we got a call that the mom was on her way to the ER. Three hours after that, we learned the baby had been delivered at 26 weeks and had not survived. The mother was crushed, and Kalle and I were heartbroken. What good could come from this?

Our adoption journey is unique because it's

ours. I know we have many other friends and family members that have experienced similar heartbreak. The realization that I was unable to give my wife a thing she has dreamed about for her entire life was equally heartbreaking. Infertility is a weird thing. It doesn't really make sense. In several places the Bible says that children are a gift, part of God's blessing to us, a reward even. What if you can't have children? Does that mean God doesn't want to bless you? When you grow up in a culture like mine, where it seems like everyone gets married and has kids before they can legally drink alcohol, it can be difficult to reconcile the truth that your story will be different than all the rest. It can make you feel like you don't belong.

The following January, two months after we had lost our boy, I flew home to Salt Lake City after attending my second week-long intensive at Boston University, and discovered that our Young Life area was beginning to struggle financially. After several meetings with our local committee, we all realized that it would be impractical for Kalle and I to continue on as *full-time* staff. We decided to pass along all direct ministry to two of our younger volunteers who would go on part-time staff. This would put less of a financial strain on the area budget and ensure that Young Life College at Utah would continue. Unfortunately, this would also mean I would be out of a job.

Kalle and I began to pray for the Lord to reveal what our next step might be. I spent several days surfing the Internet, searching for ministry jobs in Salt Lake City, thinking I could stay on Young Life staff part-time while also working for a church or non-profit. After a painful phone interview with a local church, asking me to consider the position of Middle School Director, I decided I should try another approach: solitude and prayer. I came home one afternoon to Kalle crying on the couch. "What are we going to do? We just bought this house and I don't want to move again," she said. I honestly had no idea. We both continued praying constantly, hoping the Lord would give us a way forward. The next day I got a surprise phone call.

I took the call because I recognized the area code. 509, that's Washington state. I assumed it was another telemarketer but thought it was worth a shot. "Hello," I said. The guy on the other end of the line said, "Hi Mark, you don't really know me, but we met several years ago at a Young Life camp. My name is James and I'm calling about a job opportunity for you and Kalle." (Well isn't that convenient!) James went on to share that his church was searching for two college pastors and he believed we were perfect for the jobs. James had no idea that Kalle and I were about to become unemployed. "I know you love what you get to do in Salt Lake," he said. "And I'm sure you're going to say no, but I had to try." I explained our situation to James and we spent a few minutes in prayer together. We knew that if this was God's deal, then God would figure out the details.

Kalle and I took a few days to pray and process, and a few days later we decided this opportunity *could* actually be God's provision. So, we planned a visit for the following month. It wouldn't hurt to at least check it out. I mean, we did not want to leave SLC, but we were certainly willing to go anywhere the Lord leads. A few weeks later we arrived in Ellensburg, WA for our "official visit." We toured the church, met the staff, explored the town and I even preached at the college service. Everything felt right and so natural; we all had a lot of peace about moving forward. At the end of our visit there the church offered us the jobs, making it clear to us that they all believed we were the perfect fit for this ministry. We gladly accepted, and we went back to SLC to start packing.

Our first summer in Washington was stressful (learning a new job is never easy), but after several weeks we were in a rhythm and beginning to build relationships with a lot of new students. Most of our time was spent preparing for our weekly college service, planning for events and our two annual retreats, as well as meeting with students in one-on-ones for coffee. Those meetings with the students were our favorite part of the job! We got the chance to hear their stories and about what's going on in their lives. We got to cry with them, laugh with them and walk through this messy life alongside them, sharing our own struggles and joys along the way.

I averaged anywhere from two to six coffee meetings per week. So, it didn't seem odd when I got an email from a friend asking if I'd be willing to meet with a student named John. I had never met John before. He was a sophomore at Central Washington University (CWU), majoring in business, and considering a future career in ministry. I agreed to meet with him, excited to hear more about his journey of faith. We set up a meeting for the following week at the Starbucks on campus, a favorite spot for students. I assumed most of our time would be spent swapping life stories and with

John asking me questions about what it's like being a pastor. Boy, was I wrong.

CHAPTER FIVE:

JOHN

Starbucks was abnormally busy as I stepped up to the counter to order my usual Americano with a splash of heavy cream. When John arrived, he ordered an iced vanilla latte. He mentioned that this was his favorite summer time drink and considering this was one of the hottest September months on record, this seemed like the perfect opportunity to enjoy it! We grabbed a small table by the window and began the typical small talk. Where are you from? What high school did you go to? Why did you choose Central Washington University (CWU)? How's the quarter going, and have you made any new friends? John seemed pretty easygoing and shared openly about his experiences at CWU.

John had been attending our college service for a few weeks, and he gave a gracious nod to how much he loved my style of preaching and how I always stick to biblical text. I was beginning to really like this kid! As John began to share more of his story, I could tell he had something important he wanted to say. John shared that he had grown up in a Christian home and had a close relationship with his parents, his older sister and younger brother. They went to church together every week. John had been involved in his youth group all the way through high school. He is also a musician and began writing his own songs during his Junior year of high school. His youth group even started using some of his songs for their weekly worship gatherings. Upon hearing this, I began thinking about how I could get him plugged in with the music team for our college service.

John and I had something else in common: we both loved Young Life. He had attended a Young Life retreat while in high school, and at that retreat he said he believed that God began calling him to go into full-time vocational ministry. He shared about how transformational his camp experience was, and how his Young Life leaders became like family to him.

"Young Life was like a second home for me. The first time I went to camp I was amazed at how beautiful the facility was and how happy everyone was." His smile grew, and he stared out the window longingly as he recounted his experience at Young Life camp. "My leaders joked that camp would be the best week of my life, and they were right," he said. He took another of sip of his iced latte and wiped the whip cream from his chin. "That is where everything changed for me," he said. "That's where I began to fully embrace the truth of what our camp speaker shared over and over again, that God loves me just the way I am." That's incredible, I thought. John's experience with Young Life sounded very familiar to me, as I had also been to countless Young Life camps over the previous 15+ years.

John chose to attend CWU because of their business program. CWU also happens to be one of the most affordable public universities in Washington, and it's where his parents went to college, so he'd always been a Wildcat fan. John took another big gulp of his latte and let out a big sigh before he went on. "I'd like to go to seminary after college," he said. "Since high school I've known that someday I want to go on staff with Young Life or maybe serve as a pastor at a church somewhere." This is where his story took a surprising turn.

John continued, "I knew when I graduated from college that I wanted to go on staff with a campus ministry someday. I loved attending Young Life in high school. I'd love to go on full-time staff someday. The only problem is... I'm gay," he revealed. "I know Young Life would not hire me, so I've been trying to research other campus ministries that might be open to hiring me once I graduate college. So far, no luck." I followed John's lead and went to take a big gulp of coffee, quickly realizing that my cup was empty. I was beginning to worry that my face gave away my nervous feelings. I took a deep sigh and continued with my typical '*I'm focused on you but inside I'm freaking out*' face. John tried to brush over the fact that he had just told me he was gay. I had no idea what to say so I went with, "Tell me more."

John looked down at the table and resumed. "I was 10 years old when I first realized there was something different about me. I had grown up in a church that had always said homosexuals were unnatural, an abomination. My parents knew a gay couple down the street and they would pray for them regularly to resist temptation and be saved from their immorality. One time, as we drove by their house, my mom told my dad that she hoped someday they could be cured." I listened intently as the tears began to well up in John's eyes. "I don't want to be this way. I would never choose this, and I've met with many pastors in hopes that through prayer I might change. When I turned 15, I made a promise to myself that I'd never be honest with my family or my church about being gay." John's shoulders began to slump, and he began talking more softly as he shared.

"My parents are amazing, and I know they love me. Two years ago, after battling depression and suicidal thoughts for several years, I made the decision to be honest with myself and others and 'come out' as gay. I just couldn't keep hiding this part of myself. The past two years have been brutal. I've often felt out of place with other Christians, and I have lost a lot of friends. My parents are getting better now and are at least willing to talk about it. I think they've finally realized that I can't change how I am, even though I want to. I've been praying that God would deliver me from same-sex attraction since I was 12, but my attraction to guys has only grown." John seemed like he had hit a brick wall and was ready to give up on his dream of serving with Young Life or becoming a pastor.

Perhaps like me, you may be thinking, 'How can someone like John, who grew up in a loving Christian home, who loves Jesus and has felt a call to pastoral ministry, be *gay*?' 'Is this a result of the sin in his life?' 'He must have experienced some kind of early trauma or neglect that has manifested itself this way.' 'Why can't he just pray to God and be delivered from this transgression?' 'Why can't he change if he just reads his Bible more?' Trust me, I was asking myself all these same questions as I struggled with how to respond.

I finally worked up the nerve to respond: "John, thanks for sharing this with me. I can see how hard this is for you, and I'm glad you feel safe enough to share. I'd love to know how I can help you in your process or offer you my support." John was unloading his deepest struggle with me, and I wanted to come across as patient and compassionate. But I knew what I *really* wanted to say. Those verses from the Bible began popping up in my head. Leviticus, Romans, Corinthians... You know, the ones about men lying with men and doing unnatural things? My typical pastoral answers wanted to jump out of my mouth. Things like: 'John, if you keep praying God will deliver you from this sin.' 'John, you know what the Bible says, right?' 'John, the Bible is clear on this issue. There are at least six verses that speak to this.' 'John, God never gives us more than we can handle.' But I held my tongue. I knew I had to keep my mouth shut for now. This meeting was for listening.

John went on to share that he had thought about applying to Young Life staff last year but had heard that simply because he was attracted to men he wouldn't even be considered (I'm not sure how accurate this is, but it's what he was told by another Young Lifer). I guess he was right. He heard the same thing about Campus Crusade and Intervarsity, two other large evangelical Christian para-church ministries that worked on college campuses. I asked if he had considered working for the Methodist Church, the Lutheran Church, or another denomination that affirmed LGBTQ+ Christians? He said he had considered that, but he had grown up in the Evangelical tradition and had hoped there might be a place for him there. "I grew up in a large non-denominational church, and I love the worship and the teaching. I'm also not a fan of the traditional, liturgical style of worship. I just love ministries like Young Life, and I'd give anything to be able to work for them."

Words escaped me as I began to ask the Lord how I could respond in a loving way to John's heartfelt plea for help. What was there to say? First David and now *John*. Why was God bringing these people into my life who are gay and Christian? Why were LGBTQ+ people all of a sudden showing up and wrecking my theological convictions? I was also struggling to reconcile John's passion for Jesus and the fact that he's gay. He clearly isn't *choosing* to be gay. So, if he's not choosing to be gay, and he feels called to be a minister, why should he be excluded? My head was spinning.

My phone rang as I drove back to the office. It was Kalle. I answered, "Hey babe, what's up?" She hesitated as if something was wrong. I asked again what was going on, beginning to worry. She talked slowly: "Did you know that Tiff was leaving her campus ministry job? Frank texted me this morning and said she's done at the end of this month." I had no idea. Tiff had worked in campus ministry for more than 10 years and she absolutely *loved* her job. "Why is she leaving," I asked? Maybe she found a better job with higher pay? Or maybe she had decided to go back to school or move back home, I thought? There was a pause on the line. I could almost hear the heaviness in Kalle's spirit on the other end of the line. "She has to leave because she came out as gay."

I was officially freaked out at this point, and the next day I shared with Kalle about all the crazy experiences I'd been having lately. I had the sense that God was up to something, but I was also suspicious, wondering was it just a coincidence that in the past several weeks I'd met two LGBTQ+ Christians? Not to mention one of my oldest friends from campus ministry had just come out as gay! Seeing as I hadn't knowingly met an LGBTQ+ Christian in the first 33 years of my life, this was all coming as a bit of a shock to me now.

We went to bed that night a bit shaken. I had a dream that I was sitting on a bench and someone was talking to me. I couldn't see the person who was talking but I could clearly hear what they were saying: 'Mark, choose the hard road. Choose the hard road.' What? I don't like to do hard things. I woke up in a sweat, unable to go back to sleep. The next morning over coffee I told Kalle about my dream. "What do you think that means," she asked? "Choose the hard road." We were about to find out.

For the first time in my life, I had gay friends. Moreover, my gay friends were also Christians. This was blowing up my long-held stereotypes, and these new relationships had forced me to begin doing my own research around homosexuality and the Bible. I was reading everything I could get my hands on, and I discovered that many brilliant theologians had spent decades researching this topic and had concluded that it's not so black and white. This is a complicated issue that involves some *serious* study. I knew I had to dive in! No longer were LGBTQ+ people a category in my mind, now they were friends who were hurting and searching for answers. My journey of discovery had officially begun, and my eyes and heart were quickly being opened to a bigger view of God and a more beautiful and robust view of the Bible.

CHAPTER SIX:

SHARON FROM FALL RETREAT

The October leaves were a bright orange and yellow and the Fall quarter was well under way. I had been meeting regularly with John for a couple of months, and I had also been reading everything I could get my hands on that was related to the issue of LGBTQ+ inclusion in the church. My perspective had begun to shift as I realized that there were lots of differing views on this topic. In fact, in the past 10 years many well-respected Evangelical pastors and theologians had begun changing their views based on recent psychological and biological discoveries regarding sexual orientation and gender identity (Tony Campolo, David Gushee, Jen Hatmaker, James Brownson, to name a few). I knew this was a divisive topic that many Christian churches were wrestling with, and I wondered if our college students would have an interest in discussing this.

We were only days away from our Fall Retreat where we would take more than 100 college students to a camp in Central Oregon. The weekend would consist of field games, club meetings, meals in the dining hall, dance parties, late night events, a concert and very little sleep. I thought our Fall Retreat would be the perfect opportunity to host a question and answer session with students. A few days before we left, I sent out a survey to students, so they could anonymously submit any question they hoped to address during our time together. No surprise, one question came up *way* more than any other: "Is it a sin to be gay?" This was the one thing that every student was dying to talk about. They all had friends who were gay, and they had all been told by our church that it's a sin.

I had invited my friend Rod to come as our guest speaker for the weekend. Rod is a college professor, and he had agreed to co-lead our question and answer time with me during the weekend. The Q&A session began with less threatening questions like, 'What are the different types of Biblical translation?' and 'Where did the Bible come from?' Rod and I were seated on the stage in two big cushioned chairs. I had even set a side table up and a floor lamp to make it look like a living room. More casual, I thought. We were having a blast and after about 20 minutes I could tell that most students were engaged, so I went for it. "So, Rod, here's an interesting question that came up more than any other question on this survey: If being gay is a sin, then why does God make gay people?" The room fell silent, and I'm pretty sure the temperature rose about 30 degrees in an instant. Is it just me or is it roasting in here? Here comes the sweat again. You could have heard a pin drop. Students were on the edges of their seats waiting for Rod's response. He was our camp speaker, a well-respected Evangelical pastor and scholar. If anyone could help answer this question, it would be Rod, right? Rod took a deep breath: "Mark, I actually don't believe that it *is* a sin to be gay."

All of a sudden, I felt a weight lift off of my shoulders. It was as if the heavens opened up and Jesus himself came floating into the room. I can't explain it, but I knew in that instant that I fully agreed with Rod. Being gay *isn't* a sin. Rod had just confirmed my newly formed belief, based on months of prayer and study, that it's not a sin to be gay. Suddenly, I had the urge to shout from the stage that any LGBTQ+ person in the room should feel fully welcomed and affirmed! The freedom I felt was overwhelming. The only problem was, I may have been the only person in the room besides Rod that agreed with his response. How would the *students* respond to Rod's answer? What would they say when they got home and people from our conservative church began asking questions? What would they think when they found out that I *agreed* with Rod? Better yet, what would my supervising pastor think? How much longer would I have a job?

Playing it cool, I responded to Rod's statement: "Wow! That's so interesting. I know there are several views on this issue, and I'm sure there are some folks here who are surprised to hear you say that it's not a sin to be gay." Rod continued, "This is a complicated issue that I'm afraid our Christian culture has often gotten wrong. Not only have we gotten it wrong, but Christians have done a lot of damage along the way. Our Biblical literalism has caused harm to LGBTQ+ individuals who are searching for a place to belong." I couldn't believe Rod was saying this from on stage. Most of the students in the room believed that homosexuality was wrong, and I knew we would be facing lots of questions at the end of this Q&A time. Boy, was I right.

For the next two weeks I was constantly meeting with students, taking phone calls from adults in the community and having conversations with other pastors about the conversations we'd had at Fall retreat. People couldn't believe that our camp speaker had said from stage that it's not a sin to be gay. And they especially couldn't believe that I had agreed with him! During most of these meetings I explained why I had agreed with Rod and began trying to help other people understand *why* I believed the issue of homosexuality wasn't so black and white. Many of the people I met with had little desire to hear my thoughts on this topic, and some people got downright pissed. Others, however, were grateful that we had broached this topic and were eager to learn more. While each meeting was important, one particular conversation would end up changing everything.

One week after Fall retreat I got a text message from Sharon. I had met Sharon at our weekly college service before the retreat, and she had mentioned she wanted to meet with my wife and me. We couldn't make it work before the retreat, and now Sharon was adamant. Her text message said that she had to meet AS SOON AS POSSIBLE. Apparently, this was regarding something that was said at Fall retreat and it COULDN'T WAIT.

Sharon was a senior at CWU and had been a regular attender and volunteer at our Tuesday night service. Kalle and I had even considered asking her to join our leadership team next year. She was super smart and outgoing with a great smile, and we knew she would be a welcoming presence to any new guests. I texted her back and we agreed on a time to meet. The next day Sharon was sitting in my office with tears in her eyes. What *now*, I thought?

The first snow of the year had just blanketed the ground in Ellensburg, and Sharon was slumped down in a chair in my office. She was hiding in the hood of her down jacket. Kalle sat next to me and quietly asked Sharon to share about what was going on. We both knew bits and pieces of Sharon's story. Specifically, we knew she had recently found out that a close family member had cancer. I assumed she was still wrestling with the implications of this and how to best support her family during this difficult time. I wasn't prepared for what she said next.

"I've been thinking lately about ending my life," she said. "I've tried to harm myself before, and the counselor that my parents forced me to see hasn't been able to help. The other day I actually came up with a plan" (They don't prepare you for these kinds of conversations in the seminary). Maybe I should tell Sharon to go next door to see our Lead Pastor? I'm sure he's much better equipped to deal with this. Better yet, our care pastor down the hall was also a police chaplain. Surely, he knows how to handle this type of crisis. But alas, Sharon had asked to meet with Kalle and me. She was inviting us to join her on this journey. "Sharon, I'm so sorry," I said. "Can you tell us about what's going on? Can you share the kinds of thoughts that have led you to want to hurt yourself?" That's the best I could come up with. She went on.

"Since I can remember, I've struggled with same-sex attraction. I think I'm gay." Sharon went on to share that ever since hearing me talk about homosexuality at Fall retreat, she had been dying to meet with me. She said there was no one in her life that she could talk to about this. Her mom had *insisted* that these feelings of same sex attraction were just a phase and that she needed to resist these sinful temptations. For years people had clobbered Sharon with the few verses from Scripture that *seemed* to condemn any homosexual behavior. She now had them memorized. This, however, didn't change the fact that she was attracted exclusively to women. These thoughts, and the inability to share them with anyone in her life (not to mention the fact that being gay would exclude her from fully participating in the church that she loved), had led her to try and take her own life. This was just too much for her to bear. This was also becoming too much for *me* to bear.

Thankfully, Kalle chimed in, "Sharon, we love you and we are so thankful you felt safe enough to come and talk to us. Have you been able to pray about this? Do you sense God's presence in your life? What is God saying you to?" Sharon began to cry. "Kalle and Mark, I grew up going to church and my family is very religious. I know all the right things to say and do. I desperately want to have a relationship with God, but I know I'm not worthy. I know that I can't follow Jesus *and* feel this way. I've decided that based on what my pastor says and what the Bible says, faith in God is just not for me." My heart sank as she shared.

I sat speechless in my office chair. I couldn't imagine what Sharon was going through. Since she was 10 years old, she had been told that what she was feeling on the inside was inappropriate and unnatural. She had been told that she must change, or *else.* Her parents had condemned her feelings and her thoughts, and she was now feeling impossibly isolated and alone. Sinking into a pit of despair in my own mind, I decided to ask a provoking question: "Sharon, how are you feeling now, after Fall retreat?"

"Mark, before Fall retreat I had never heard a Christian say that it's not a sin to be gay. Much less a Christian *pastor*! When you said that from up front I began to feel a sense of hope and felt free for the first time...maybe ever." My mind was racing as I attempted to understand what I had just heard. Sharon felt free... because a Christian pastor told her that the feelings she had (feelings that she couldn't control) were okay... that maybe God made her this way... and maybe God loves her this way? The pieces began falling into place in my mind. There was no going back now. After months of prayer and study, and countless conversations, I was realizing that God was doing something incredible, showing me a bigger view of the Bible and a bigger view of God. I was now *convinced* that LGBTQ+ individuals should be fully welcomed and affirmed in the church, just the way they are. And I was almost ready to share it with the world, no matter the consequences.

CHAPTER SEVEN:

WHAT DOES THE CHURCH SAY?

* Warning – I am a faithful and committed follower of Christ who has spent the past ten years studying theology, first at Fuller Seminary and now at Boston Univ. I am not claiming to have all the answers, but I, like you, am on the faith journey. In the coming weeks, I will be introducing a new theological perspective on the issue of LGBTQ+ inclusion (as revealed to me through study and prayer). If you are not open to considering a new perspective, this may be where you get off the bus. Go in peace.

There were several inches of snow on the ground the next morning when I met with one of my supervising pastors. We sat in his office with warm cups of coffee in hand, both wearing heavy flannel shirts and snow boots. We made small talk for several minutes, and then I shot in. The question was burning inside me. I just had to know. "Pete why aren't we allowed to baptize gay people?" Pete shifted in his chair, almost spilling his coffee on his leg. "Well, I honestly don't know much about the issue, and I'm not sure there's any *formal* policy. But I do know that unless they remain celibate, and turn from the homosexual lifestyle, that we definitely can't baptize them and allow them to join the church. It's really the same as any other sin." I took a deep breath.

This answer wasn't cutting it for me anymore. So, basically any LGBTQ+ individual that wished to be baptized and join the church just had to commit to being alone for the rest of their lives? I could see Sharon's face in my mind. I could picture John with tears running down his cheeks and David as he shared about his love for God and his passion for pastoral ministry. I had made new friends whose stories complicated this issue, and I wasn't satisfied with this typical Evangelical response anymore. I pressed in on the issue. "Pete, I know there are a *couple* places in the Bible where it *hints* at homosexuality being a sin. Is that the final answer on the issue? There's no room for discussion?" Pete looked out his window. I could see the wheels spinning in his head. "That's it. I mean the Bible is the final authority for us, ya know? And it's pretty clear in Scripture. It's tough but we can't deny the truth of God's word."

I could tell even he wasn't quite satisfied with his *own* answers at this point. He went on, "Look, let's keep talking about this. I'll do a little digging and you do the same. Let's see if there's some wiggle room here. Honestly, I'm probably not the best person to ask anyway. I'm definitely not an expert on this topic." I began to wonder how we could deny *baptism* to someone and not even have a firm grasp on *why*? I left Pete's office that day on a mission to communicate how this policy of exclusion was inconsistent with Jesus' ministry of radical *inclusion* as we see it throughout scripture. I knew there was more to the story than the few highly-debated verses from the Bible. Now I had faces in my mind of people who had suffered because of our teaching around this issue. Not only that, but I was beginning to build my own case against the traditional Biblical teaching the excludes LGBTQ+ individuals from participation in the church.

All Kalle and I had talked about for several months was LGBTQ+ inclusion. It's all I could think about. I had read at least ten books on this topic written by prominent evangelical theologians, and I spent countless hours poring over the various passages in the Bible. I was reading every translation, in English, Greek and Hebrew, not to mention other ancient literature, trying to get to the bottom of what the Bible *really* says about homosexuality. If I was going to have this conversation with my supervisors and other leaders in our church, then I had to know *how* to dialogue about this issue. The greatest catalyst for my new-found passion were these new friendships, and now God was leading me to advocate for our new friends that had been suffering for too long.

One day, as Kalle and I were talking at our home

in Ellensburg, she had a revelation. We had spent the past two years struggling to understand how difficult life was for our LGBTQ+ friends, and suddenly she proclaimed, "Wait! I'm not gay. I will never understand what it's like to be gay. How could we ever tell someone that *is* gay that they're wrong? Who are we to tell them how they should *feel*?" This sounds obvious, but that day it seemed to strike a nerve with both of us. This seemed to be a new approach to the conversation. How had we been so blind to the experiences of others? Or perhaps, more likely, we had been blinded by the traditional stance of our church, and we were just now beginning to see things through a new lens?

Why had it taken me so long to take a hard look at LGBTQ+ inclusion? Had I been avoiding this issue because it made me uncomfortable? Perhaps it was because I didn't *fully* understand why the church was excluding LGBTQ+ individuals, or know how to explain it? Or perhaps it was because, until now, I had never really taken the time to build a genuine relationship with a gay person, or someone who is transgender? I had never listened to their stories and tried to see things from their perspective?

In my experience, a large majority of my evangelical Christian friends that oppose LGBTQ+

inclusion in the church don't actually *have* any close relationships with LGBTQ+ Christians. Nor have they spent much time studying this topic. We fear what we don't know. The moment I began listening to the stories of my new friends, the desire to understand their perspective began to grow inside me. What was their life like? What was it like being told by people you love and respect that you don't fully belong because of the way you're made?

We met with a friend the following day for lunch at our favorite little spot in town. As we ate we began discussing this topic (because it's basically all we ever talk about now). Our friend attends the Methodist church in town and they are what evangelical Christians call "open and affirming." This means that LGBTQ+ individuals are fully welcome to participate, serve, become ordained and be married at the church. Our friend shared a simple illustration that began to help me see this issue from a different perspective:

"Think of it like this," she said. "Imagine we are all walking on the sidewalk, and all of a sudden the two of us trip on a big rock. We look at each other. You seem unfazed, but the pain in my foot is so great that I can't help but cry out." She took a sip of her coffee. "You look me in the eyes and say, 'Come on! That doesn't hurt. You're not really feeling pain in your foot.' But how can *you* know what I'm feeling? In fact, it doesn't matter what you *think* I'm feeling, it only matters what I'm *actually* feeling. I'm the only one that gets to decide if something is painful." I realized this was an oversimplification of the issue, but it started to make sense. Who was I to think that I could tell someone how they feel about another person? It's not up to me. How silly would it be for me to tell her in that moment, as her foot was throbbing in pain, that according to my personal manual on foot injuries, that type of injury should not be causing her any pain?

I was beginning to realize that I had merely been regurgitating what I had been told my whole life, growing up in the conservative South, working for evangelical organizations and now an evangelical church, and attending an evangelical seminary. Most people that I had spoken with from our church regarding this issue were not even interested in having a conversation. They were not even willing to consider a different perspective. This seemed odd to me because those same people had most likely never even taken the time to study this topic. I'm talking about taking an in-depth look at the Bible in its original languages, studying the cultural context and the intent of the authors. Also, remembering that God is *alive*, and the Holy Spirit is living and active among us, guiding us as we seek to faithfully interpret and apply scripture in order to love God and others.

No longer was I afraid to share with others about what I'd been learning. I began meeting students for coffee and telling them about my experiences and about my new friendships. On several occasions I had openly shared with other staff members at our church about what I was learning. People now knew that Kalle and I fully affirmed LGBTQ+ individuals. The weird thing was... no one wanted to talk to us about it. It felt like we had disappeared. That is, until I shared with our new Senior Pastor about our position on this issue. He was *all* ears.

CHAPTER EIGHT:

DISRUPTION

* Disclaimer – The following posts are riddled with proof-texts (i.e. extracting individual verses to promote or support a personal viewpoint). In order to focus on the major themes of the Biblical scriptures I typically try to avoid proof-texting, but for the purposes of this post referencing individual verses helps provide clarity.

When I sit down with someone to talk about LGBTQ+ inclusion now (and I've had countless conversations on this topic), the conversation normally goes something like this:

FRIEND: "Mark, how can you think that it's *okay* to be gay? It's pretty clear in Scripture that it's a sin."

ME: "Really? Where exactly does it *clearly* say that in Scripture? Actually, faithful committed same-sex relationships were likely a foreign concept to the authors of the Biblical texts. Many scholars agree that they were writing specifically about sexual idolatry. Regardless, it's certainly not *clear*."

FRIEND: "Well, I know there's something about homosexuality being an abomination in Leviticus...or is it Judges? Either way, I know it's in there. And I know Paul says it's wrong too. Just read that one verse in Romans. Also, God made males and females. That's clear according to science."

ME: "Yeah, well the truth is, it's not black and white. It's a complicated issue, and there are so many questions about the context and culture surrounding those few verses that you're referencing, and many theologians believe it's possible that none of those verses are *actually* referring to faithful monogamous same-sex relationships. Lots of smart people believe the questions outweigh the answers regarding the history and meaning behind those passages. There are a few books I'd recommend if you want to check it out for yourself. What do you say?"

FRIEND: "Wow. Well... I'm not sure I'd trust those *liberal*s who write *those* kinds of books. Anyway, maybe I will research it a little more someday, but for now I have to trust what my pastor says."

ME: "That's fine. But if you ever want to find out for yourself, just know that there are some brilliant people with new and healthy perspectives on this incredibly important topic. Ultimately, I'd encourage you to pray and ask the Lord to reveal the truth about God's heart for LGBTQ+ individuals. More importantly, ask God to bring some LGBTQ+ Christians into your life to share their own stories with you. Remember, God is bigger than the Bible. God is alive and doing new things all the time in our world! Isn't that reassuring?"

That's usually when the conversation ends. "Check, please."

In January, my pastor and I met to discuss this topic, and he was anxious to hear about where we stood. Thankfully, at this point I had met with lots of people to explain our new discoveries, and I was getting pretty good at sharing how Kalle and I had come to this conclusion. However, he wasn't too interested in hearing *how* we came to our conclusion, or even about our research. He was more interested in hearing about how this new perspective might be received by the church board and other members. That's understandable.

Our initial meeting went well. He was open to my perspective and conceded that our views might be more consistent with the views of our college students, which would allow us to grow our reach on campus. He said he admired my passion for theological study, and he was aware that this was an important topic that we should all try and learn more about someday. I assured him that I had spent the better part of two years researching and praying about God's heart on this topic. More than what we think the *Bible* might say regarding this issue, I had been seeking the truth about what *God* says concerning LGBTQ+ inclusion. I hadn't come to this conclusion lightly, and I was excited about the new relationships we'd been building as a result of our newfound openness. He seemed optimistic and I was ecstatic that we would get to keep our jobs and continue ministering to college students at CWU.

The next day, however, he called me back into his office. After giving it a little more thought, and after chatting briefly with another board member from our church, he realized that he couldn't budge on the issue of LGBTQ+ inclusion. He said that according to the church's policy (and the views of the denomination) this was a deal-breaker. He asked Kalle and I to either uphold the church's policy of prohibiting LGBTQ+ students from serving... or leave. When I pressed the issue, asking if we might be able to meet with the board and share more about our perspective and our heart behind why we came to this conclusion, his response was clear: "No, that's not an option. This issue really is black and white."

At the end of February, we were given an

ultimatum: we could keep our jobs and prohibit LGBTQ+ students from fully participating in the college ministry or we could leave. Seeing as we had just been led down this path of new life by God's great hand of grace, understanding the truth of God's diversity and inclusiveness, we knew we could not compromise on our theological convictions. We had to leave.

* Sidenote: The church was incredibly gracious throughout our resignation process. Our pastor even apologized on behalf of the leadership, as he realized that this issue should have been discussed before we were hired. While we did not want to resign, we all realized that this was not the best fit for us, and everyone involved was respectful of these differing views. All in all, our departure was healthy which we are thankful for!

I had hoped that we could begin to dialogue about this issue with the church staff and board of elders. Couldn't we all sit down and talk openly about this topic, consider different views and perspectives and pray together as a community of faith about this issue that has caused so much harm to LGBTQ+ individuals? I mean, this issue is not *resolved* by any means. In reality, the topic of LGBTQ+ inclusion in the Christian church has caused many scholars to scratch their heads for decades. Also, in the past twenty years, science has begun to catch up with us and we finally know the truth: LGBTQ+ individuals cannot change the way they are. Sexual identity is core to who we are as human beings, and so is our sexual orientation.[1]

When my pastor informed me that neither he nor our board of elders were interested in hearing a different perspective on this topic, I began to wonder why. There *is* another perspective worth considering. When Kalle and I invited the Holy Spirit to guide our process, opening our minds to a new and different perspective, our minds and hearts were transformed. We prayed every day for a year that if we were wrong about this that God would help correct our views. Instead, God continued to guide us down this path towards inclusion, inspiring our biblical study and bringing new friends into our world.

One of the most convicting realizations that I experienced on this journey came when I was

---

[1] For those who support conversion/reparative therapy, you should note that Exodus International, an Evangelical organization that was focused on "curing" homosexuals, shut its doors in 2011 after 30 years of operation. Their president, Alan Chambers, admitted a 100% failure rate. They were never able to alter any patient's sexual orientation. You can read more here: https://www.theatlantic.com/politics/archive/2015/10/the-man-who-dismantled-the-ex-gay-ministry/408970/

meeting with Sharon (remember Sharon from Chapter 6?). She was in the middle of explaining how she had tried to deny her own sexual orientation since she was about 10 years old because she was being told by her parents and her church that she was "unnatural". When she realized she couldn't change who she was, she tried to take her own life. She couldn't live with the fact that every time she saw a pretty girl and experienced that release of oxytocin (oxytocin is a hormone that is released in the body when we experience physical or sexual attraction, which we have no control over), she was filled with guilt and shame. What if Sharon had the freedom to enjoy a faithful monogamous relationship with someone she is attracted to, just like any heterosexual person?

Think about this: When you met your husband or wife, or significant other, did you make a *conscious* decision to be *attracted* to that person? NO! You just *were*. It's no different for someone who is attracted to individuals of the same sex. They experience the same kind of attraction. And guess what... we don't get to tell other people who *they* are attracted to. We don't get to decide how someone else *feels*.

* Sidenote – We also don't get to mandate celibacy. Celibacy is a unique and personal

calling. What is more accurate is to say that we are all "called" to companionship as revealed in Genesis 2:18 (Interestingly, the word we translate as 'partner' or 'companion' here is actually a masculine noun in the Hebrew, 'E'zer', which is also used to refer to God throughout the OT). I've received many emails from people saying there is a "third way." In other words, "Mark, we don't have to 'exclude' or 'affirm', we can just tell LGBTQ+ individuals that as long as they remain single/alone, it's all good! That's pretty rough logic, as any limitation on inclusion is simply exclusion. Not to mention the fact that this contradicts God's proclamation that it's not good for us to be alone. No more trying to mandate celibacy, please.

I know, I know... I've heard the same old arguments countless times: "Well then, based on your arguments, should we just let murderers keep on murdering because they *feel* like it, Mark?" I think we are all intelligent enough to understand the difference between killing another human (or embracing a sexual addiction, or cheating on your wife, etc...) and making a lifelong commitment to love and serve another human. There is a *clear* difference between causing harm and choosing to live in a faithful union with another individual, which reflects God's heart for covenant relationship, mutual respect and love.

Let me briefly say, if you are one of those individuals who is willing to argue for the exclusion of a certain group of people, let's go ahead and make sure we get the whole picture. Here are a few of the "clear" statements from the Bible about how Christians *should* live (and these are just the ones that kind of make sense for us in today's culture, excluding the verses that prohibit eating shellfish and child sacrifice, etc...): Love your enemies (Matt. 5), give to *everyone* who begs from you (Luke 6), do not judge one another (Luke 6), it is not lawful for men to divorce their wives (Mark 10), take nothing for your journey (Luke 10), give food to the hungry, welcome the stranger (alien, immigrant) as you welcomed me (Lev. 19:34), take care of the sick, visit prisoners (Matt. 25), and my personal favorite: sell **all** your possessions and give to the poor (Mark 10). Why aren't there more Christians who have taken a vow of poverty?

How are there Christian pastors (like myself) that live in nice houses and drive nice cars? How do Christians justify living a middle-class (or upper-class) lifestyle while so many people in the world go hungry, completely disregarding this clear biblical teaching? At the end of the day, aren't we all just picking and choosing the verses we want to live by and those we wish to ignore?

And if this is the case, how could we ever *choose*

to defend an obscure and highly debated teaching that alienates and causes harm to an already vulnerable population, in light of Jesus' own ministry of radical inclusion? Should our theology cause harm? Shouldn't we default to *inclusion* and radical love instead of moral superiority (since none of us will measure up anyway according to Paul; Romans 2:1)? Not to mention the fact that the single commandment that Jesus tells us to live by (the one that fulfills *all* the law and prophets) is to simply love one another?

The truth is, this issue requires more than a conversation around biblical interpretation. In order to faithfully engage this topic, we must learn to embrace reality. In this case, loving our LGBTQ+ brothers and sisters means paying attention to their suffering and no longer denying the reality that sexual identity and orientation is not black and white. I'm going to complicate things a bit more here and share another fascinating fact as related to the real gender spectrum: it's estimated that 1 to 2 in 2000 children born in the US are born with *both* sexual organs (This is according to an article published by ABC News, and if you're interested in learning more just Google it). These children used to be called hermaphrodites (that's considered derogatory today), now they are referred to as 'intersex'. Today, doctors are asked to choose (with the parents' approval) the appropriate gender for the child, and most perform the necessary procedure before the child is 18 months old. Unfortunately, there is a high rate of inaccuracy when choosing the appropriate gender (some estimate as high as 50% rate of inaccuracy).

Maybe you're asking yourself, "Why can't they just look at Chromosomes and choose? It's pretty straight forward isn't it?" Actually, no it isn't. Gender is truly fluid. Biological sex is determined by five factors present at birth: the presence or absence of a Y chromosome, the type of gonads, the sex hormones, the internal genitalia (such as the uterus in females), and the external genitalia. To *further* muddy the waters, the test results are not just either male or female, they can actually be on a sliding scale between the two. When doctors are unable to line up *all* of these factors, babies that grow up as female actually have the chromosomal and genetic make-up of a male, or vice versa. This can result in a tortured childhood, and when the child hits puberty this often causes visible gender confusion, which results in bullying, depression and higher rates of suicide. Unfortunately, this can be true for LGB individuals as well.

According to a recent report published by the CDC, nearly one third of LGB youth have attempted suicide in the past year. That's compared to only 6% of heterosexual youth. Sociologists and psychologists claim that these higher rates of depression and suicide are a direct result of being bullied, discriminated against, misunderstood and rejected by family and friends, and being excluded from places of worship and social circles. Don't believe me? Sit down with a LGBTQ+ individual and ask them to share their story with you.

In light of this tragic reality, how should Christian leaders respond? Should Christians *ignore* these statistics and the reality of this human suffering and continue to uphold "traditional biblical teaching" (or our denominational versions of this biblical teaching) for the sake of preserving a moral standard? Let's not forget the whole point (the overarching theme) of Paul's letter addressed to the church in Rome, that in regard to morality, we *all* fall short of the glory of God and are saved by God's unending grace. Praise the Lord!

How does *Jesus* respond to those who are suffering? Perhaps, instead of living in denial, grasping for an idealistic world where only the righteous get to decide who's in and who's out, we might begin to pay attention to the voices of those who have been marginalized and oppressed. These beloved voices might inspire us to re-examine our traditional Biblical teaching, much like we have done surrounding past issues like circumcision, divorce, women in leadership, and slavery (to name a few), in hopes of discovering a more inclusive and affirming approach? Will we take the time to listen?

In 2015, Gary Gates, a researcher at UCLA, estimated that roughly 4% of the population of America identify as LGBTQ+. This is an old statistic and also a conservative one, as many LGBTQ+ individuals remain in the closet for fear of being ostracized or condemned by their families or communities. According to this figure, there were approximately 20 students in our former college congregation of 400 who identify as LGBTQ+. Simply put, there are a lot of LGBTQ+ individuals in the US. And if you keep walking down this rabbit trail of statistics you'll find that of the 9 million LGBTQ+ individuals in the USA, roughly 7 million of those maintain some kind of Christian faith (this is based on PEW Research data which suggests that some 70% of Americans claim some type of Christian faith).

Many brilliant scholars and pastors *have* gone back to the biblical text to try and figure out if there's room for this diverse gender spectrum in the greater theological conversation. The fact is, LGBTQ+ individuals *do* exist (and there are a lot of them), and they can't change the way they are. So, is there a chance that we have misinterpreted and abused Scripture for the sake of preserving our heteronormative Christian culture? That's certainly a question that's worth asking and it certainly wouldn't be the first time. Especially considering the fact that LGBTQ+ youth are 40% more likely to attempt suicide because they feel they don't belong. This is serious, y'all.

I have witnessed first-hand the harmful effects of this traditional biblical teaching and the resulting policy of exclusion against LGBTQ+ individuals. We must understand that the Bible was never intended to be used as a tool to promote our individual ideologies and personal theological convictions (especially when they cause harm). In fact, this diverse and expansive collection of poems, songs, letters and accounts that were written by many different people (with a limited and ancient knowledge of biology, psychology, and ecology) over a span of roughly 1500 years, hand-picked more than 300 years after they were written and included in the canon, were compiled specifically to do one thing: Point us to the Christ, the one "who is all and in all" **(Col. 3:11).** This begs the question: What if God *made* us this way and *loves* us this way? What if this gender spectrum is another example of God's beauty and diversity? What if there *is* a way to uphold the authority of the Biblical texts as they were intended to be read and used, while still affirming our LGBTQ+ brothers and sisters? Oh wait... I'm getting ahead of myself.

CHAPTER NINE:

WHERE DO WE GO FROM HERE?

"It is Christ Himself, not the Bible, who is the true word of God. The Bible, read in the right spirit and with the guidance of good teachers, will bring us to Him. We must not use the Bible as a sort of encyclopedia out of which texts can be taken for use as weapons."[2]

- C.S. Lewis

For hundreds of years white European and American people used individual verses from the Bible to justify the unjust and brutal treatment of African Americans and other people of color who were bought and sold as property. It took an embarrassingly long time for us to realize that this went against the very nature of who God is, God's design of all human beings in God's image, and how we as Christians are called to treat our neighbors. Interestingly, the Bible never actually *condemns* slavery. Biblically, those who fought for slavery *were* justified. The Bible only explains *how* we should treat our slaves more fairly. So, if the Bible doesn't *condemn* slavery, then what caused Christian people in Europe and America to stand up against this horrific practice? The words on the pages of the Bible certainly never changed.

---

[2] This is a paraphrase from a letter written by Lewis to a colleague. The full meaning remains intact.

No, the primary catalyst for the abolitionist movement was that Europeans in power finally came to their senses and acknowledged that African Americans and other people of color are also made in God's image and therefore deserving of dignity and equal opportunity. And it was Jesus' stance on radical inclusion that led these abolitionists to stand up against slavery.[3] Jesus broke the pattern of historical exclusion among religious circles when he spoke out against racism and hatred towards certain tribes (e.g. Luke 4). The truth is, only when people in power, especially Christian pastors and leaders, acknowledged the atrocities of their actions were they willing to go back to the text of scripture, which they had used to *justify* slavery in the first place, and reexamine their traditional interpretation and application. They began to read scripture through the lens of Christ and his life and ministry of radical love and inclusion, which ultimately led to the abolition of slavery.

Recently, a close family member confided in me that they were wrestling with the issue of LGBTQ+ inclusion. They mentioned that they had met with their pastor and discussed this issue with

---

[3] For more on this check out Eric Metaxa's book *Amazing Grace*

her extensively. They mentioned that their pastor, a gifted female with a knack for communicating and a deep love of people, still couldn't reconcile LGBTQ+ inclusion with what's written in the Bible. I lovingly reminded my family member that it has only been in the past 30 years or so (give or take) that their pastor would have been allowed to serve in *any* position of leadership in the church in America. Despite Paul's clear acknowledgement and affirmation of female faith leaders (e.g. Romans 16) and the many women who surrounded and supported the ministry of Jesus, people have used (and still use) individual verses from scripture to prohibit women from leading in the church (e.g. 1 Corin. 14:34). Thankfully, many churches have overcome these historical stereotypes and ancient cultural norms to see a bigger picture of God and to embrace a better method for interpreting the biblical texts.

We must remember that the living God is the *ultimate* authority. The question is not, "What does the *Bible* say" but "What does *God* say?"[4] In order to

---

[4] Several critics, in an attempt to defend their perspective that the Bible is God's Word and the sole authority for our faith, have pointed out to me that a few NT authors do refer to the 'Word of God'. Let me be clear, the Bible did not exist when these accounts and letters were being written. Therefore, when the authors of the NT refer to the

faithfully discern God's purpose and meaning, we must read and interpret scripture through the lens of the life and ministry of Jesus Christ, who is "the image of the invisible God."[5] In other words, when we study the Bible, we must always be asking ourselves, how does this passage reflect God's purpose for humanity and God's revelation of Godself through the person of Jesus Christ? Jesus said that "He who has seen me has seen the Father."[6] Only when we reclaim this holistic method of Biblical interpretation will we truly arrive at the *meaning* of Scripture, discovering a new perspective that is actually more congruent with the Evangelical tradition, one that more accurately reflects Jesus' heart for *all* people.

The most responsible method of biblical interpretation is to move from a 'micro reading' of scripture towards a 'macro reading' of Scripture. In

---

'scriptures', they are largely referring to the Jewish scriptures (among other ancient sacred texts), and when they refer to the 'Word of God' (e.g. John 1), they are speaking specifically about the *spoken* word of God, God's creative order, the Logos, the Christ, and not about the Bible (look it up in your Greek dictionary). Thankfully, the Bible now serves as an invaluable tool for us today, but we must not forget that God has been living and active among us since the beginning of creation and did not just show up after the Bible was written.

[5] Colossians 1:15 NKJV
[6] John 14:9 NKJV

other words, we can't just pick and choose individual verses from scripture and use them to bolster our own views and perspectives (By the way, you can almost justify *any* worldview by using this 'proof-texting' method of interpretation). All scripture must adhere to the larger themes of the Christian faith, the common threads we find throughout the canon: grace, forgiveness, mercy, love, diversity, inclusion, etc... All Scripture must fall under the authority of Jesus Christ; his life, ministry, death and resurrection. We must continually ask ourselves, what does this particular passage mean in light of the fact that all of history is moving from, in and towards redemption through Christ? Moving further inward, we then must examine the *purpose* of each book, as written by the author to his particular context, in order to understand the meaning of each individual passage.[7]

---

[7] For example, one of the major themes of Paul's letter to the church in Rome is that we are justified by God's grace through faith in Christ. That we all fall short of God's glory, and none can boast in their actions or behavior. Another example: a major theme of Paul's letter to the church in Colossae is that there should be no division among you, that "Christ is all and in all" (Col. 3:11). We must read each sentence of those letters through the lens of their major themes. Remember, these were originally written as continuous letters, without verse numbers and section headings.

David Gushee and James Brownson are two Evangelical pastors and scholars that have courageously examined the topic of LGBTQ+ inclusion and have revisited the passages that have traditionally been used to condemn any behavior outside of heterosexual norms.[8] They have examined these passages through a more holistic "Christ-lens."[9] Their conclusion is clear: there *is* a way to remain faithful to the meaning and purpose of the biblical text, while leaving space for the affirmation and full inclusion of our LGBTQ+ brothers and sisters. If we are open to considering this new perspective, then we will be able to move towards an open dialogue regarding LGBTQ+ inclusion, moving closer to affirmation and reconciliation.

A friend of mine called me after my first blog

---

[8] There are seven primary passages in scripture that have been used in this way: Genesis 9:20–27, Genesis 19:1–11, Leviticus 18:22, 20:13, 1 Corinthians 6:9–10; 1 Timothy 1:10, Romans 1:26–27. Additionally, many people reference passages that describe the distinction between male and female as a defense of hetero-normativity (Genesis 1 and 2, Jesus' teaching on marriage).

[9] *Changing our Mind* by David Gushee and *Bible Gender Sexuality* by James Brownson ... and if you're interested in learning more about the intersection of the science of gender and the biblical text check out *Sex Difference in Christian Theology* by Megan DeFranza

post went public and asked, "Hey, I'm interested in learning more. Where do I start?" The first thing I would suggest would be to pray and ask God to guide your journey. In Acts 5:38-39 wise Gamaliel, a religious leader, offers some great advice to the Pharisees, the earliest adversaries of the Christian faith: "...if this plan or this work is of men, it will come to nothing; but if it is of God, you cannot overthrow it – lest you even be found to fight against God." If we trust God's power in our lives, then we shouldn't be afraid to consider a new perspective. Even if this new perspective challenges our traditional reading of the biblical text.

My second suggestion would be to ask the Lord to bring some LGBTQ+ Christians into your life. Take some time to listen to their stories and try to see and understand their perspective. Then, read *Changing our Mind* by Dr. David Gushee as an introduction to this journey of discovery. Dr. Gushee does a wonderful job of introducing this new perspective and he guides you as you begin to reexamine your own beliefs, while presenting a compelling case for considering a new direction. Before you do, however, you must promise to have an open mind! "How do I do that," you ask? Well, the first step is to embrace reality.

The fact is, LGBTQ+ Christians *do* exist. So, how do we reconcile this reality and still uphold the authority of Scripture? How do we remain faithful to this ancient text that we've been trying to study and understand for centuries (remembering that our interpretation and application of scripture never stops evolving) while allowing for a new perspective on LGBTQ+ inclusion? While I cannot provide a decent answer for you in a short blog post, I would say: Let this be the start of your own journey of discovery! Kalle and I have been led to new revelations of God's mystery and majesty. God is so much bigger and more diverse and beautiful than we ever imagined. The Holy Spirit brought us from a place of closed-mindedness to hearts that are fully open to embracing people that we once didn't understand. Isn't that what loving your neighbor is all about?

One thing that was clear to me as I began this journey of discovery was that this issue is not "black and white." After much prayer and research, I began to realize that this is an incredibly *complicated* issue that affects millions of lives. I know some of these people now. I also know that over the past ten years *entire* Christian denominations had "come out" and declared that they are open and fully affirming (e.g.

Presbyterian Church USA, Evangelical Lutheran Church of America, two-thirds of the United Methodist Church in America, and *even* some Baptist churches). That means some churches fully accept and affirm LGBTQ+ individuals and some do not. My question is... which side more accurately reflects Jesus' own radically inclusive life and ministry? Those that exclude or those that affirm? I just have a hard time believing that when I get to the pearly gates Jesus is going to look at me and say, "Hey Mark, I really wish you had been harder on the homosexuals. Couldn't you read the *Bible* and realize how much I hate same sex marriage?" That's just not the Jesus we see in the scriptures, and that's not the Jesus I know.

CHAPTER TEN:

WHO SPEAKS FOR GOD?

"Is there a reliable guide to when we are really
hearing the voice of God, or just a self-interested or
even quite ungodly voice in the language of
heaven? I think there is. Who speaks for God?
When the voice of God is invoked on behalf of
those who have no voice, it is time to listen. But
when the name of God is used to benefit the
interests of those who are speaking, it is time to be
very careful. The crucial difference is who benefits
from the voice of God being spoken and heard."

- Jim Wallis, *Who Speaks for God?*

Jesus never stands with those in power. Throughout
the New Testament, we never see Jesus defending
the interests of the religious elite. We never see him
fighting to protect religious institutions or
traditions. In fact, he repeatedly speaks against
these institutions and traditions in order to advocate
for the marginalized. Moreover, the only people
Jesus ever seems to condemn are the *religious*
leaders. When Jesus is confronted by the Pharisees
in their many attempts to deceive him, he *always*
sides with the powerless, the oppressed. Off the top
of my head:

Jesus invites poor and uneducated fishermen
and blue-collar workers to be his closest
companions and disciples, he cleanses the lepers
and the demon-possessed (who have been outcast
by mainstream society) and restores them to their

rightful place in the community, Jesus openly forgives and empowers a woman caught in adultery and a woman guilty of promiscuity (requiring no penance), he forgives and blesses prostitutes and thieves, he praises the good Samaritan that crosses cultural and socio-economic boundaries to radically love a brother in need, asking nothing in return. I could go on.

We can trust the voice of God only when that voice is leading us to love the least of these. Who is benefiting from the voice of God being spoken and heard? If we are preaching a message that promotes upward mobility, increasing our wealth and securing our personal and national borders, then we are not preaching the gospel of Christ. If we are preaching a gospel message that does not guide us deeper into the forgotten corners of society, standing in solidarity with the oppressed, then we are not preaching the gospel of Christ. Has the church grown too comfortable, insulated in our fancy buildings, preaching a gospel of moral superiority, while those whom God longs to love are forgotten and relegated to the margins of society? My friend Lina says, "The gospel is not good news unless it's good news for *everyone.*"

I would argue that for our LGBTQ+ brothers

and sisters, a message of "Be single or be excluded"
is not good news. A message of "Unless you live up
to *our* moral standard, you will not be permitted to
answer God's calling on your life to serve **God's**
church" is not good news. A message of "I get to
decide what God is speaking into *your* life, based on
my reading of Scripture," is not good news. Christ
did not promote a gospel of moralism. Christ
preached a gospel of grace and radical acceptance.
Today, I believe Christ would stand in solidarity with
our LGBTQ+ brothers and sisters who have been
misunderstood, misrepresented and marginalized.

Two weeks ago, I asked this question: should our
theology cause harm? We can clearly see, if we are
willing to open our eyes and pay attention to the
reality of the hardship that many LGBTQ+ individuals
face on a daily basis, that our traditional theological
perspective has caused immense harm (this is
undeniable). Thankfully, the apostle Paul writes
specifically to this question in his letter written to
the church in Rome:

"Owe no one anything, except to love one another;
for the one who loves another has fulfilled the law.
The commandments, 'You shall not commit
adultery; You shall not murder; You shall not steal;
You shall not covet'; and any other commandment,
are summed up in this word, 'Love your neighbor as
yourself.' Love does no wrong to a neighbor;

therefore, love is the fulfilling of the law."
– Romans 13:8-10 NRSV

Have we fulfilled this law? Are we truly upholding Christ's commandment to love one another as we fight to exclude those we do not fully understand? Shouldn't we read all of scripture through this lens of love? Shouldn't this lens of love supersede our attempts to use scripture to draw lines of morality in the sand? Perhaps the voice of God *is* speaking but we are slow to listen for fear that our comfortable and convenient Christian cultural norms might be disrupted? That is a question that you must answer for yourself, hopefully as you sit in the presence of the Christ, who *is* love.[10] Should our theology cause harm, or should our theology draw people into the gracious embrace of God's Kingdom?

Maybe you're wondering how the rest of our story unfolded? Well, two days after we resigned from our jobs I began emailing everyone I knew, sharing my resume and sending sermon links. Though I did receive some interest, there were no clear open doors or opportunities. My new theological convictions posed a challenge for me as

---

[10] 1 John 4:7-12

an Evangelical pastor and faith leader. Who in my large network of Evangelical faith leaders would hire a pastor that *affirms* LGBTQ+ individuals?

A week had passed when I received an email from our friend Jen who was at the time the senior pastor at Ellensburg First United Methodist Church (EUMC). She expressed her full support for us, and she committed to pray for our upcoming transition. She also shared a bit of classified information: She was leaving her position as Senior Pastor at EUMC in July. She asked if I would ever consider stepping into such a role? Kalle and I smiled and said we'd 'pray about it'.

Well, we *did* pray about this potential opportunity. We also forgot about it. Until several days later when I got a phone call from Pastor Jen. Her call could be classified as a miracle. She asked if I wanted to take the next step in the hiring process? I laughed it off, thinking I could never do anything like that. I'd never even been to a Methodist Church service. I'd never been a senior pastor. I'd never officiated a wedding or funeral. Wouldn't they want a seasoned Methodist minister? Surely there were more qualified candidates? I said yes, and the next thing I knew I was on a phone interview with two district superintendents and a few church members.

Two months after leaving our jobs as college pastors at a church where LGBTQ+ individuals are prohibited from serving, I was *leading* a church service alongside an elder at EUMC, an LGBTQ+ individual who is a faithful follower of Christ and a well-respected leader in this community. This person is now one of my good friends and partners in ministry. And, as if God's miracle couldn't have been any *clearer*, the church also happened to be hiring a college minister, and they promptly invited Kalle to apply for *that* position.

Five months later, Kalle and I are still serving alongside one another, preaching and teaching the truth about God's radically inclusive and grace-filled love for all people. We are following God's leading in our lives, growing in our awareness of God and growing in our understanding of what the Bible *is* and *how* to faithfully and responsibly interpret and apply it to our lives. Please come visit us at Ellensburg First United Methodist Church. I preach most Sundays, and I occasionally help out with music. And, yes... *All* people are *fully* welcome at our new church. And let me say, God is present and active among us in this diverse community of believers, and there is a richness and authenticity here unlike anything I've ever experienced. Perhaps that's because we have attempted to embrace the journey of discovery and been led to a deeper well of grace and truth?

As a word of encouragement for those who are considering this new perspective and wondering how it will affect your life and work and community... know that it will. You will suffer, and you will hurt if you decide to stand in solidarity with your LGBTQ+ brothers and sisters (just imagine how *they* feel). You will lose friends and you will lose respect from other Christians (how ironic). Let me say, as someone who has been through the ringer recently... it's totally worth it. The journey of following Christ is a journey of downward mobility, as we are led into the depths of the pain and suffering that Christ suffered for us. Following Christ is not easy, the road is narrow, and the way is difficult. Why should we expect anything different?

Shalom.

CHAPTER ELEVEN:

RESPONSE TO CRITICS

From a reader:

"The tradition of the last 2000 years would be more reliable than the sudden shift of those "evolving" in the last 19 years. Really sad."

My response:

Hey, thanks for posting! Evolution can be defined as "the gradual development of something, especially from a simple to a more complex form." I think we can all agree that human sexuality, or at least our understanding of human sexuality has "evolved" over the past 2000 years. For example, we now know that roughly 1% of babies born in the world are born with both sexual organs, and we now know that transgenderism and homosexuality are not "mental disorders" as they were thought to be in the mid-late twentieth century. These are scientific facts that were unavailable to the authors of the Biblical texts. Are we to ignore these facts and discoveries and attempt to create our sexual ethic based on the cultural norms of ancient Israel? Or should our "evolution" in thought and scientific discovery lead us to reexamine our Biblical teaching, much like we did on the issue of circumcision or slavery? The Bible never actually condemns slavery, it only tells us how to treat our slaves. The words on the pages of the Bible never changed, we just realized that African Americans and people of color are human beings that deserve respect and equality.

....

From a reader:
Intentionally accepting "unrepentant sin" is wrong, no matter the translation/version of the Bible you're reading. The cultural bias argument you're attempting to make is essentially an excuse to ignore what Scripture calls sin, for the sake of acceptance and being politically correct.

My Response:
Thanks for your comment! I'm curious what else you would classify as "unrepentant sin?" What is your Biblically-derived ethic regarding materialism, greed or pride? Those are very clear in Scripture. I myself, as a straight white male would have to admit that I too am living in unrepentant sin based on the fact that I live in a large house and am among the top 1% of the wealthiest people in the world because I get paid a living wage (while millions of others go hungry). Additionally, Jesus himself actually corrects the Jewish scriptures on several occasions ("You've heard it said...well I tell

you...), placing marked contradictions within the pages of our Bible. I guess the point I'm trying to make is that this is no simple issue and there are many respectable perspectives that are worth considering. In fact, most of the issues that we white, privileged Westerners like to think are cut and dry are highly debated among theologians and scholars from around the world. The issue of LGBTQ+ inclusion would be one of those. Thanks for engaging!

....

From a reader:
I know I won't change your mind, so I won't even try, but just curious... did you come to where you are today based on reading the Bible?!?!? If you lived on a deserted island and the Bible washed up to shore... what sexual ethic do you think the Bible would teach as you read it?!?"

My response:
I've heard some version of this response countless times before. People saying things like: "Okay, so you affirm LGBTQ+ individuals now. I guess you don't believe the BIBLE anymore?!?" That couldn't be further from the truth, and it's also a gross oversimplification of the issue. My first question to

my friend would be: "Which version of the Bible washed up to shore? Was it the original Greek or Hebrew (of which I would have no idea how to translate)? Oh, and if it was the Greek or Hebrew there would be MANY missing words and phrases from those original documents of which I would have to do my best to fill in the gaps (like every Biblical translator has admittedly done for centuries…that's why there is a disclaimer written by the translators at the beginning of most Bibles that says something along the lines of "We did our best to fill in the missing gaps and we hope we got it close based on the information we had.")

Or was it the first English version of the Bible which was a translation that was commissioned by King James in the 17th Century? This was written for the wealthy English and translated by a group of wealthy elite white Englishmen (but I'm sure they had no level of personal or cultural bias and could be completely objective in their language selection). Not to mention the fact that Bible was largely unavailable in languages other than Greek, Hebrew or Latin before the Reformation. This meant that prior to the 15th Century only language experts had access to the words on the pages of the Bible. Oh, and by the way, there are thousands of people still today that will never have access to a Bible. Are we supposed to believe that their only access to knowledge of God is through Scripture? Do we really believe that God is so small?

But back to the point... today we are privileged to have many different English translations of the Bible. So, my question again would be... which translation washed up to shore on this deserted island? Was it the NIV, the NKJV, the NRSV, the MSG, the YLT, the AMPC, the AMP, the CEB, the CEV, the CJB (there are dozens more by the way)? Beyond that we must consider what my hermeneutical lens might be. Am I Jewish? Reformed Jewish? Eastern Orthodox Christian? Presbyterian? Methodist? Non-denominational? Catholic? Roman Catholic? Once we determine all of these factors, then I can answer your question: "What sexual ethic do you believe the Bible would teach you as you read it?" My answer, depending on all of the above-mentioned factors would be drastically different, as many Presbyterians, Methodists, Reformed Jewish, Catholics, Eastern Orthodox Christians, etc... all agree that LGBTQ+ individuals should be fully affirmed in the Christian church, based on their experience of the living God and their interpretation of Scripture. Which then begs the question... who's right and who's wrong? And which side more closely reflects the radically inclusive ministry of Jesus Christ?

....

From multiple readers:
Many people have questioned my views on the reliability of the biblical text.

My response:
The Bible is the written account of the ancient Jewish and Christian people and their inspired experience of God. The Bible is the *written* revelation of God, filtered through the human capacity to hear from and understand God. The Biblical texts lay a foundation and set a trajectory for our Christian faith and practice, which is continually evolving and expanding. One of my favorite Biblical scholars, Richard Rohr, likes to say that the Bible is "the word of God in the words of men." In other words, the authors of the Biblical text were regular people like you and me. They wrote from a particular place in history, saw through a particular cultural and socio-economic lens, and they had a limited understanding of biology, psychology and ecology. The authors of Scripture were primarily concerned with telling

113

their version of who God is and who they were, which would ultimately inform our own journey. Is the Bible inerrant or infallible? Well, now that is the great debate. It's interesting to note that the Bible itself never claims to be inerrant or infallible. The concept of Biblical inerrancy is a modern concept that was introduced by conservative Christians in the 19th Century as a defense against modern or progressive Biblical interpretation (mainly combating recent scientific discoveries). Many of those conservative theologians also claimed that we must interpret Scripture *literally*. This, however, becomes a problem when we try to make literal sense out of books like Leviticus, for example. Unless you are still in the habit of sacrificing goats? And Mosaic law from the book of Exodus becomes problematic, unless of course you are going to institute slavery back into our system. Simply stated, we no longer live in ancient Israel, and we now have a greater understanding of ourselves and the world.

Thus, we now read and interpret Scripture through our *own* historical-cultural lens. This doesn't mean the Bible has nothing to offer us in how we should live our lives, but it does require a greater understanding of the historical and cultural context within which the Scriptures were written in order to faithfully and responsibly apply them today. When we do not have a firm grasp on *what* the Bible is and *how* the Bible should be used, humans tend to *misuse* the Biblical text, choosing individual verses in the Bible to support and defend our own personal ideologies or political positions. History has proven that this type of Biblical interpretation causes immense harm (e.g. slavery, segregation, anti-Semitism, etc...). So how then should we read and interpret Scripture?

In John 5:39, Jesus himself reminds the religious leaders that they will not find Truth *in* the Scriptures, but the purpose of the Scriptures themselves are to point *to* Christ! Therefore, we must read and interpret all of Scripture (Old and New Testament) through the lens of the life and ministry of Christ. All of history is moving from, towards and in Jesus, who is fully God and fully human. The writer of Hebrews proclaims, "The Son is the radiance of God's glory, and the exact representation of God's being." While the Bible is authoritative for the purpose of understanding the history of the practice of the Christian faith, all of scripture must ultimately fall under the *supreme* authority of the person and work of Christ. Jesus was clear, if you want to see and understand who God is and what God is like, look at me.

Thankfully, when Jesus ascended into heaven he did not promise to leave us The Bible. He promised to leave us the "advocate" or God's spirit. We must learn to trust the work of the Holy Spirit in our lives and in the lives of others.

If you're interested in learning more about my perspective, check out Richard Rohr's *Things Hidden* or Peter Enn's *How the Bible Actually Works*. Also, one of my favorite podcasts is called *The Bible for Normal People*.

....

From a reader:

I said this in an email to you earlier, and I'll say this publicly now. The lens you are removing is a conservative one, but you wear multiple lenses. Let those reading this blog consider, are you really just a product of "conservative, Christian upbringing?" Is that truly what the West is today? Or are you also a product of a culture with a progressive, liberal, sexually free worldview? Neither is necessary all good or all bad, but I would submit that nearly all the readers of this blog have strong influences from both sides of our culture and that those lenses affect how they read scripture in ways that tend both liberal and conservative at various times.

Mark, you have made the case that you have taken off your lenses, that you are willing to set aside dogma. I don't doubt this journey has been honest and authentic, but I question how much you have really removed your liberal, modern/postmodern lenses as well. It's worth noting that your own denomination didn't sanction same sex marriage because of the global footprint of the UMC. To be honest, it sounds a lot more white male American thing to do to claim that you know best when your black and brown brothers and sisters globally are saying otherwise. Implicitly you are arguing that our global church leaders, the vast majority of whom hold to a conservative position on this issue, are wrong and need corrected by their American and European friends. That could be, but I would tread lightly. History has shown we (white, male, westerns) are often wrong on its wrong side, as you cited above with slavery.

Mark, you have made the argument that God would not deny to people their romantic and sexual attraction. But let me ask you: don't we all deny our romantic and sexual attraction throughout our lives? When I said yes to my wife, didn't I say "no" to all the others that I will be attracted to in the future? Didn't I say "no" to them prior to marriage as I waited for a monogamous relationship? Is it really outside Christ's character then that he would say no to desires deeply felt? Further, do you counsel your young people to avoid premarital sex? If you reject the proof texts above, how can you make an argument from scripture that premarital sex is wrong? You can't, because there are even fewer than those prohibiting same sex relationships. If we're rejecting individual prooftexts for a wholistic, grand view of scripture, doesn't it seem in keeping with God's plan of redemption that he is a God of grace and loves when we feel loved? Thus, if you feel loved when you are sleeping with your girlfriend that's probably what he wants for you or at least is willing to look the other way on? I'm fully aware I will not convince you, you haven't entered into this lightly and have come to your conclusion. Having read to the end, I would like my above comments to at least posted to present another perspective. Thank you.

My response:
Thanks so much for your engagement and for your respectful criticism these past few weeks. I

understand your concerns, and I believe that I have made it clear that I'm not condoning sexual promiscuity. The problem we are facing in our world today is that people somehow equate homosexuality with sexual promiscuity. Being gay and in a relationship does not equal sexual promiscuity. We do see clear teaching against sex outside of the bonds of a faithful monogamous relationship. I have made that clear throughout these past few weeks.

You're married, right? I am happily married, and I came to a difficult realization a couple years ago when I began this journey of discovery. As a married man, it seems a bit hypocritical for me to tell someone else that they have no right to enjoy the level of intimacy and love experienced in a faithful union that I have enjoyed with my wife, based on my interpretation of the Bible. Perhaps it would make sense if you and I were without any sin in our lives, to cast that stone of exclusion against LGBTQ+ individuals. Again, it's important to pay attention to the voices and views of our LGBTQ+ Christian brothers and sisters who live with this reality every day and who are also attempting to live as faithful followers of Christ (I have several books I could recommend if you're interested in their perspective).

If I was living a holy and blameless life, then perhaps I could more easily justify the notion that my job as a Christian pastor is to manage the behavior of others. However, that's not my reading of the text and that's not my understanding of the calling of Christ on my life. My understanding is that we are called not to manage the behavior of others but to invite all people to enjoy the beauty and wonder of a relationship with Christ, learning to recognize and trust the presence and work of Christ in others and responsibly guiding them into a healthy view of scripture.

My goal, as stated from the first chapter, is not to "be right." My goal is to encourage others to begin their own journey of discovery, being led by the spirit into a more robust and inclusive view of God and the biblical text.

GOD IS BIGGER THAN WE THINK

EPILOGUE:

For you who have loved Jesus – perhaps with great passion and protectiveness – do you recognize that any God worthy of the name must transcend creeds and denominations, time and place, nations and ethnicities, and all the vagaries of gender, extending to the limits of all we can see, suffer and enjoy? You are not your gender, your nationality, your ethnicity, your skin color, or your social class. Why, oh why, do Christians allow these temporary costumes, or what Thomas Merton called 'the false self,' to pass for the substantial self, which is always 'hidden in Christ with God' (Colossians 3:3)? It seems that we really do not know our own Gospel. You are a child of God, and always will be, even when you don't believe it.

- Richard Rohr, *Universal Christ*

NOTES

_____

_____

_____

_____

_____

_____

_____

_____

_____

_____

_____

NOTES

_____

_____

_____

_____

_____

_____

_____

_____

_____

_____

_____

NOTES

NOTES

_____

_____

_____

_____

_____

_____

_____

_____

_____

_____

_____

NOTES

NOTES

_____

_____

_____

_____

_____

_____

_____

_____

_____

_____

_____

NOTES

_____

_____

_____

_____

_____

_____

_____

_____

_____

_____

_____

NOTES

_____

_____

_____

_____

_____

_____

_____

_____

_____

_____

_____

ABOUT THE AUTHOR

Rev. Mark W. Wagner has been traveling the world sharing stories for more than 14 years. He has traveled to 15 countries and most states in the United States as an accomplished singer/songwriter. He holds a Master of Arts in Theology and Ministry from Fuller Theological Seminary and is currently completing his Doctorate in Transformational Leadership at Boston University. Mark serves as the Senior Pastor at Ellensburg United Methodist Church in Ellensburg, WA where he lives with his wife Kalle Marie. He has self-published three books that are available on Amazon.

Other books by Mark W. Wagner,
available on Amazon:

Desert Day

*An invitation to solitude and renewal from
Psalm 23*

POPPY

*The biography of William Hugh Haney, my
grandfather*

Learning to Lament

*A framework for honest expression using
Psalm 13*

You can also listen to Mark's music on all
digital streaming services.

www.markwagnermusic.com

INVITE MARK

If your church or organization is interested in exploring the issue of LGBTQ+ inclusion, Mark would love to come visit and help you begin to facilitate a healthy dialogue around this important topic.

Mark has shared at countless retreats, conferences, church services, staff meetings and other events around the world, and he is a skilled communicator and facilitator.

If you're interested in booking Mark for your event, contact him here:

markwesleywagner@gmail.com

For more information on the experiences of
LGBTQ+ youth visit the Trevor Project:

www.trevorproject.org

For more information on how to advocate for the
inclusion of LGBTQ+ individuals in the church visit
The Reformation Project:

www.reformationproject.org

GOD IS BIGGER THAN WE THINK

51600899R00088

Made in the USA
Lexington, KY
04 September 2019